EXPLOR
LIFE
CYCLES!

KATHLEEN M. REILLY
ILLUSTRATED BY BRYAN STONE

green press
INITIATIVE

Nomad Press is committed to preserving ancient forests and natural resources. We elected to print *Explore Life Cycles!* on 96% post consumer recycled paper, processed chlorine free. As a result, for this printing, we have saved:

18 Trees, (equal to 0.4 American football fields)

11,014 Gallons of water, (equal to a shower of 2.3 days)

2,563 Pounds of air emissions, (equal to emissions of 0.2 cars per year)

Nomad Press made this paper choice because our printer, Transcontinental, is a member of Green Press Initiative, a nonprofit program dedicated to supporting authors, publishers, and suppliers in their efforts to reduce their use of fiber obtained from endangered forests.

For more information, visit www.greenpressinitiative.org

Nomad Press
A division of Nomad Communications
10 9 8 7 6 5 4 3 2 1
Copyright © 2011 by Nomad Press
All rights reserved.

This book was manufactured by Transcontinental Gagné,
Louiseville Québec, Canada
March 2011, Job #43197
ISBN: 978-1-934670-80-4

Illustrations by Bryan Stone
Questions regarding the ordering of this book should be addressed to
Independent Publishers Group
814 N. Franklin St.
Chicago, IL 60610
www.ipgbook.com

Nomad Press
2456 Christian St.
White River Junction, VT 05001
www.nomadpress.net

Contents

Other titles from Nomad Press in the **Explore Your World!** Series

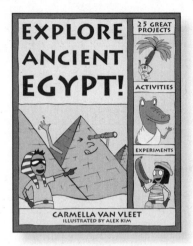

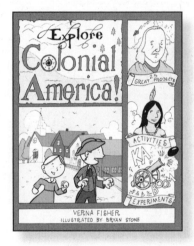

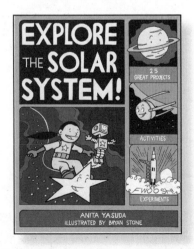

Introduction

Have you ever planted a garden with your parents? You cover the seeds with soil and water them. A few days later a little green shoot pokes out of the ground. Within weeks, the little green shoot transforms into a flower, vegetable, or fruit.

Or maybe you once owned a kitten or puppy. It's amazing how fast they grow from a tiny little fur ball into a young animal with tons of energy. Before you know it your kitten or puppy is a full-sized cat or dog. You might have also had the sad experience of losing a beloved pet who grew old and died.

WORDS TO KNOW

stage: a single step in a process.

life cycle: the full life of a living thing, from birth to death.

habitat: the natural area where a plant or an animal lives.

These are all **stages** of life. Every living thing goes through them. Together, these stages are called the **life cycle**.

Different creatures go through different changes during their life cycle. For example, a toad begins life as a swimming tadpole before growing into an adult. A butterfly starts out as a caterpillar before transforming itself. A huge oak tree begins life as a tiny acorn that slowly grows over many years. And you start out as a tiny infant!

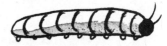

All living things may grow differently, but they all follow the same basic stages of the life cycle.

In this book, you'll explore all these stages. You'll see how plants and animals go through each stage. You'll also find out what happens when something disrupts a life cycle—like acid rain or the destruction of **habitat**.

But most of all, you'll have fun as you tackle projects and activities that explore these ideas. So turn the page and let's get started with the cycle of life!

An Endless Cycle

Can you remember what it was like when you were younger? You were smaller, sure. And you probably couldn't do many things that you can do now. Maybe you couldn't ride a two-wheeler yet, or write a thank-you card, or climb the monkey bars at the playground.

Now imagine what you'll be like 20 years from now. You'll be an adult. Maybe you'll even have kids of your own!

WORDS TO KNOW

organism: a living thing, such as a plant or animal.

species: a group of plants or animals that are related and look the same.

Everyone goes through a lot of different stages in their lifetime. All **organisms** grow, change shape, create new life, and die. Then the life cycle begins all over again.

HEY! WHERE DID YOU COME FROM?

Did You Know?

Most animal species lay eggs! For every 100 animal **species**, 3 give birth to live young and 97 lay eggs.

All organisms begin life in a certain way. But the ways they begin can be very different. Some organisms begin life inside their mothers. Others start inside seeds. And some begin inside eggs. It all depends on the species.

4

An Endless Cycle

It's not just the start of their lives that can be different, either. An entire life cycle can also be very different. An adult mayfly may only live 30 minutes. But a quahog, which is a kind of clam, can live about 200 years. That means that a quahog that's alive today was born long before the invention of electricity.

The length of individual life cycle stages can differ, too. Some organisms grow much faster than others. For example, a human mom grows her baby inside her for 9 months—but an elephant grows her baby for 22 months! A human baby takes about 18 years to reach adulthood. But a puppy takes about one year.

← MAYFLY

HERE I AM, WORLD!

It's a special moment when new life comes into the world. It might be like when you were born, greeted with a big celebration. Or it might just be a new little blade of grass that no one notices. But all life is a truly amazing thing. It's what makes our planet special in the entire solar system.

The name of the first stage of life depends on the species. For example, humans are babies, dogs are puppies, and plants are seedlings. Many new creatures are completely helpless, like human babies or kittens. Others can stand within an hour of being born, like a baby giraffe. Some newborn creatures are almost completely able to take care of themselves, like a newborn shark.

GAME ON!

The next stage of the life cycle is focused on growing and learning skills. Human babies learn how to control their own arms and legs. Wild animal babies learn how to **forage** for food and respond to danger. Plants aren't really "learning" anything at this stage, but they grow stronger as their roots go deeper into the ground and they start getting larger.

WORDS TO KNOW

forage: to search for food.

photosynthesis: how plants turn sunlight and water into food to grow.

BIG LEAGUES

Adulthood is the next stage of the life cycle. This is where most organisms spend most of their lives. They're fully grown, and doing the things they need to do to live their lives.

For people, this is when they'll most likely be working, pursuing hobbies, and meeting someone they want to marry. For animals, this is when they'll be seeking food and shelter, finding a mate, and not getting eaten themselves! And most plants spend this time doing their job— something called **photosynthesis**. This is the way they convert sunlight to food.

During this stage, organisms usually create new life, too. Birds lay eggs, horses have foals, and oak trees drop acorns that become new trees.

WRAPPING IT UP

The final stage of the life cycle is when the organism dies. For people, we think of this as something that's really sad. But even though we don't like to think about it, death is a very natural part of the life cycle. And the life cycle itself can never die or end.

MAKE YOUR OWN
Life Cycle Möbius Strip

The cycle of life keeps going on and on. You can play with this idea by using a clever invention called a Möbius strip. It was named after the person who created it.

HMM...

1 You'll need a long strip of paper, about 2 inches wide. To make it long enough, cut two strips of the same width from the long side of your paper and tape them together. Make sure you tape it all the way across the width of the paper.

2 Decorate both sides of your paper with pictures of an organism's life cycle.

3 Lay the paper on the table. Mark the upper left corner of the paper "A." Write "B" on the lower left corner. Label the upper right corner "C," and the lower left corner "D."

4 Pick the paper up with both hands. Give the paper a half-twist, and bring the "AB" side over to meet the "CD" side. You want the A to touch the D, and the B to touch the C.

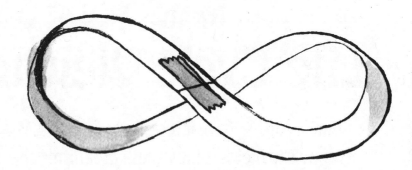

- paper (8½ x 11 is fine, but longer is even better)
- scissors
- tape
- pen, crayons, or markers

5 Tape the paper together where the ends meet. You now have a Möbius strip.

6 Lay the strip on the table. Put your pen on the middle of the inside of the strip. Without picking up your pen, slowly pull the strip so that you make a line right down the middle. Keep going until you meet your starting point. You'll not only go around the whole inside of the strip, but the outside, too—without picking up your pen!

7 Carefully cut along the line.

What's happening?

You don't get two strips—you get one even longer Möbius strip! That's just like the cycle of life. It keeps going on and on. If your new strip is thick enough, you can draw another line down the middle and cut it again and again until it's too thin.

Activity

MAKE YOUR OWN
Life Cycle Viewing Strips

Some creatures have interesting life cycles. Make a life cycle viewing strip to show others how these organisms change over time.

Supplies

- ❀ egg cartons
- ❀ scissors
- ❀ green construction paper
- ❀ glue
- ❀ dried peas or very small, round beads
- ❀ clay
- ❀ pipe cleaners
- ❀ uncooked bowtie pasta
- ❀ paint or markers
- ❀ string
- ❀ small google eyes

1 Cut the egg cartons into strips so you have rows of three cups. Each cup will represent a different life stage.

2 To make a butterfly life cycle, cut a small leaf out of the green construction paper. It needs to fit in the egg cup. Carefully glue several dried peas or beads to the leaf. These are the butterfly's eggs. For the second cup, roll three small balls of clay and attach them together. Snip off two pieces of pipe cleaner to stick into the head for antennae. This is your caterpillar stage.

Activity

3 For the third cup, cut a piece of pipe cleaner and glue it to the middle of a piece of uncooked bowtie pasta. This is the butterfly. You can use paint or markers to decorate your butterfly life cycle.

4 To make a frog life cycle, paint the inside of your first cup blue to represent water. Glue in beads or dried peas for the frog's eggs. In the second cup, make an oval-shaped ball of clay. Stick a short string into one end to make your tadpole.

5 For the frog, roll two balls of clay, one bigger than the other. Stick them together with the larger ball on the bottom. Slightly flatten the top ball to shape the frog's head. Press google eyes onto your frog. Make legs out of pipe cleaners. Put your frog in the third cup.

Keep it going:

Think of other organisms you can do. A plant goes from a seed to a seedling to an adult flower. A mealworm changes from an egg to a worm to a beetle.

MAKE YOUR OWN
Nature Quest

Whether you live in the quiet countryside or the bustling city, you're surrounded by organisms moving through their life cycles. In this project, you can create your own nature quest. You can even ask your parents to take you to a park, forest, or beach to go on your quest.

Supplies

* pad of paper (unlined works best, but you can use paper with lines)
* pencil or pen
* measuring tape
* camera (optional)

1 Make three columns on your paper. Label the first, "Living Thing." Label the second, "Life Stage." Label the third, "Details."

2 With your parent's permission, take your supplies and head outside. Take your time—if you're rushing down the street or through the forest, you're going to miss a lot.

3 When you see a living thing that interests you, stop. Is it a fern? The neighbor's cat? A bird?

4 In the first column, write down what you've found.

5 For the second column, consider the organism. If it's the neighbor's cat, is she a kitten? Or a slow-moving older cat, lazing in the sun? If it's a fern, can you tell if it's a new sprout? Or is it fully grown? If it's a bird, does it have a nest nearby? Look around for one. See if you can identify which life stage the organism is in. Write it down in the second column.

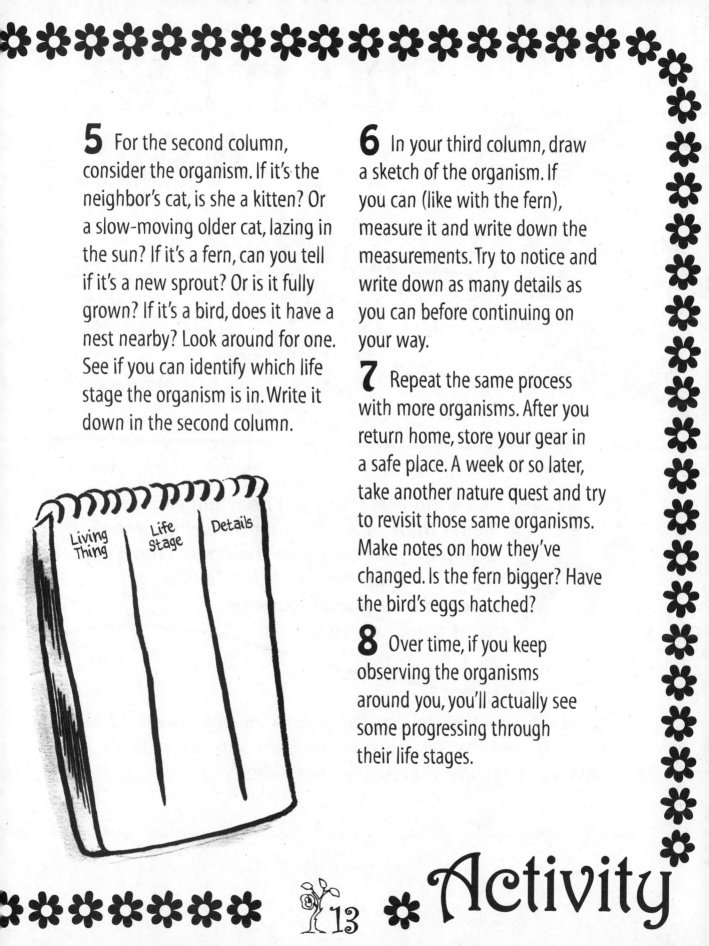

Living Thing | Life Stage | Details

6 In your third column, draw a sketch of the organism. If you can (like with the fern), measure it and write down the measurements. Try to notice and write down as many details as you can before continuing on your way.

7 Repeat the same process with more organisms. After you return home, store your gear in a safe place. A week or so later, take another nature quest and try to revisit those same organisms. Make notes on how they've changed. Is the fern bigger? Have the bird's eggs hatched?

8 Over time, if you keep observing the organisms around you, you'll actually see some progressing through their life stages.

Activity

DOES IT HAVE A FACE?

What's the first thing you do when you get home from trick-or-treating on Halloween? Dump all your candy on the floor! Then you might separate the candy into a pile of chocolate, a pile of lollipops, a pile of gum, and so on.

You could even sort it further. For example, the chocolate pile could be divided into chocolate with nuts, chocolate with peanut butter, or solid chocolate. What you're really doing is **classifying**.

Did You Know?

Scientists identify living things by sorting them into smaller and smaller groups:

Kingdom ↓

Phylum ↓

Class ↓

Order ↓

Family ↓

Genus ↓

Species

classify: to put things in groups based on what they have in common.

When scientists classify living organisms, they separate them into groups based on things they have in common. They might classify organisms based on the way they look. Or they might classify them based on common life cycles.

You can tell that animals are different from plants. Animals can move and think. Plants can take the energy from the sun and turn it into food. This is a process called photosynthesis. So scientists divide plants and animals into two different groups. These groups are called kingdoms.

Beginning with these two main kingdoms, scientists then break things down even more. Animals can be classified as mammals or birds, for example. And plants can be classified depending on whether they have wood bark or green stems.

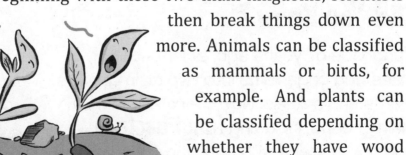

15

WORDS TO KNOW

fungi: the plural of fungus.

bacteria: tiny organisms found in animals, plants, soil, and water.

cell: a small unit of a living thing.

WHAT ELSE IS THERE?

There are other kingdoms besides plants and animals. The fungus kingdom includes mushrooms. These are different from plants because they don't have roots or perform photosynthesis. Other organisms in the fungus kingdom are mildew and mold. Mold is the green or white stuff that grows on old bread.

If you went diving deep in the ocean, you might see oysters, sponges, and shrimp. Each of these organisms belongs to a different group within the animal kingdom. And see those beautiful pink and orange rocks over there? Those aren't really rocks—they're living creatures called coral. Yep, you guessed it—another family entirely.

Did You Know?

Hundreds of years ago, scientists only classified organisms into two main groups: plants and animals. Now there are more main groups, including **fungi, bacteria,** and tiny critters with only one **cell.**

WE'RE ALL DIFFERENT

So what does classifying organisms have to do with life cycles? Organisms are often classified into groups depending on their particular life cycles. All organisms share the same basic stages—birth, growth, adult life, and death. But the way they go through those stages is often very, very different.

Consider these different life cycles:

Stage	*FROG*	*HUMAN*	*OAK TREE*
Birth	*Begins life inside an egg*	*Begins life inside their mother*	*Begins life inside an acorn*
Youth	*Swims around underwater as a tadpole*	*Develops from a baby to toddler to child*	*Grows as a small, green seedling*
Adult Life	*Transforms into a frog that lives on land*	*Stops growing after around 18 years*	*Grows bark and keeps growing larger each year*

TIME FOR YOUR CLOSE-UP...

If you were to study the life cycles of every species, you'd be studying for a really long time. Scientists have identified 2 million species so far. But they think there are between 5 and 100 million different species on Earth. Most just haven't been identified yet!

2 MILLION IDENTIFIED SPECIES

UP TO 100 MILLION SPECIES NOT IDENTIFIED

Many of the species on Earth have similar life cycles. All mammals follow the same general cycle, for example. So do fish. Let's take a look at some of these different life cycles a little closer.

MAMMALS

Mammals are a class of animals in the **phylum chordata**. This is a large group of animals that have spinal cords. A mammal is a creature that has a backbone and fur. It produces milk to feed its young. Humans, dogs, horses, whales, and mice are some mammals.

BIRTH: Most mammals grow their baby inside the mother. They give birth when the baby is ready to live outside the mother's body.

GROWTH: Usually, mammals only change in size. They get bigger until they reach their adult size, and then they stop growing. But sometimes there are other small changes. Dalmatian puppies start out all white. As they get older they get dark spots.

BIRDS

Birds are also a class of animals in the phylum chordata. A bird is a feathered creature. It has a backbone and lays eggs. Most birds fly, although there are a few birds that don't fly, like ostriches and penguins. Tiny hummingbirds and large **emus** are all in this group.

BIRTH: Like fish, birds lay eggs. But the eggs of birds have hard shells. Inside this protective home, the baby grows until it's ready to break out.

GROWTH: When birds first break out of their shells, they have fuzzy down feathers that aren't good for flying. As they get older they grow flight feathers. Some birds also change color. The bald eagle is brown all over as a youth. It gets its white head and tail feathers when it's an adult.

WORDS TO KNOW

phylum chordata: a large group in the animal kingdom. It includes mammals, birds, fish, reptiles, and amphibians. These animals all have spinal cords.

emu: a large bird with strong, fast legs that can't fly.

monotreme: a mammal that lays eggs.

Did You Know?

Some mammals lay eggs! This kind of mammal is called a **monotreme**. An example of a monotreme is the platypus.

FISH

Like mammals and birds, fish are a class of animals in the phylum chordata. A fish usually lives its entire life under water. Fish have backbones and breath through **gills** instead of lungs. Tuna, sharks, and goldfish are all part of the fish group.

BIRTH: Fish produce their young by laying squishy eggs.

GROWTH: Like mammals, most fish just get bigger as they age.

INSECTS

Insects are a class of animals in the phylum arthropoda. They do not have backbones. An insect has six legs and **antennae**. Its hard body is divided into three sections. Ants, wasps, grasshoppers, and ladybugs are all in the insect family.

BIRTH: Insects hatch from tiny eggs.

GROWTH: Different kinds of insects go through different life cycles. Some insects are born and then simply grow larger. Others change dramatically in a process called **metamorphosis**. You'll read more about this in Chapter Three.

Did You Know?

Spiders aren't insects! They are in a class with scorpions, called arachnids. They have eight legs, not six legs like true insects. But spiders are arthropods, like insects.

Does It Have a Face?

AMPHIBIANS

Amphibians are in the phylum chordata. They have backbones. An amphibian begins life in the water, breathing through gills like a fish. As it grows, the amphibian begins to breathe in air like a bird or mammal. Frogs and salamanders are amphibians.

BIRTH: Amphibians start life inside jelly-like eggs. These eggs have to stay moist at all times. Usually, they're laid in water.

GROWTH: Young amphibians change from wiggly tadpoles that swim in the water to an adult with legs. Adult amphibians live mostly on land and have lungs to breathe air.

PLANTS

Organisms in the plant kingdom use photosynthesis to create their food and grow. Plants have roots and leaves and they are everywhere. Green moss clinging to rocks in the mountains is a plant. Colorful **aquatic** plants grow in the ocean.

BIRTH: Plants start from a seed.

GROWTH: After sprouting from a seed, the seedling grows into a larger, adult plant.

 WORDS TO KNOW

gills: filter-like structures that let an organism get oxygen out of the water to breathe.

antennae: a pair of organs on an insect's head that help it sense, or "feel," its surroundings.

metamorphosis: the process some animals go through in their life cycle. They change size, shape, and color.

aquatic: living or growing in water.

21

FUNGI

Organisms in the fungus kingdom "eat" by taking in **nutrients** through their surface. Although fungi look like plants, they're not. They don't have roots or leaves. They also don't make their own food, like plants. Mushrooms, mold, yeast, and mildew are all part of the fungus kingdom.

BIRTH: A new fungus grows from a spore. Spores are different from seeds because spores don't have any stored food. Spores need better conditions to get started. Fungi produce a lot of spores to have a better chance of producing more fungi.

GROWTH: Fungi grow quickly from spores into full-size organisms. They can grow just about anywhere.

There are many, many other classifications of organisms besides these. So many, in fact, that this book would have to be much thicker to cover them all! These are more groups that include organisms like earthworms, jellyfish, and **algae**.

That's one of the things that make living on Earth so interesting—there are so many different kinds of life!

WORDS TO KNOW

nutrients: the things in food and soil that organisms need to live and grow.

algae: a plant-like organism that turns light into energy but does not have leaves or roots.

MAKE YOUR OWN
INSECT LIFE CYCLE SNACK MIX

Supplies

* ½ cup peanuts
* bowl
* soft pretzels from the freezer section
* microwave
* knife
* fruit leather
* small pretzel sticks

1 Put the peanuts into a medium-sized bowl. These are your insect eggs.

2 To make caterpillars, heat up one of the soft pretzels according to the package directions. When it's ready, take it out of the microwave and break off a piece about 2 inches long. Carefully make a slice into the dark brown outside and peel it away from the soft, white inside. This is your caterpillar! One soft pretzel can give you about 10 good-sized caterpillars. You can make them smaller if you want to. Put your caterpillars in the bowl with the peanut eggs.

3 For the butterflies, cut pieces of fruit leather about 3 inches long and 1 inch wide. Lay a pretzel stick in the middle of the leather and tie the leather around the pretzel. Leave the ends loose to form the butterfly wings. Make as many butterflies as you like and put them in the bowl with the eggs and caterpillars. Toss it all together and your insect life cycle mix is ready to eat!

Activity

MAKE YOUR OWN
MEALWORM NURSERY

Mealworms are the **larvae** of grain beetles. This is the worm stage that they stay in for a couple of months. Then they enter a **pupa** stage where they don't eat. They sleep while they transform into adults. The pupa stage lasts a couple of weeks. You can watch your own mealworms go through these life stages with this nursery.

Supplies

- ❀ small jar or clear plastic container with a lid
- ❀ dry leaves or cardboard egg carton
- ❀ dry oatmeal
- ❀ apple or orange slice
- ❀ mealworms from a pet store or bait shop

1 Poke some holes in the top of your container. Crunch up the dried leaves or shred up a piece of egg carton and put it at the bottom of your container. This will be the bedding for the mealworms.

2 Scatter some oatmeal on the bedding and a small slice of apple or orange to feed the mealworms. This is your mealworm nursery.

Activity

egg stage

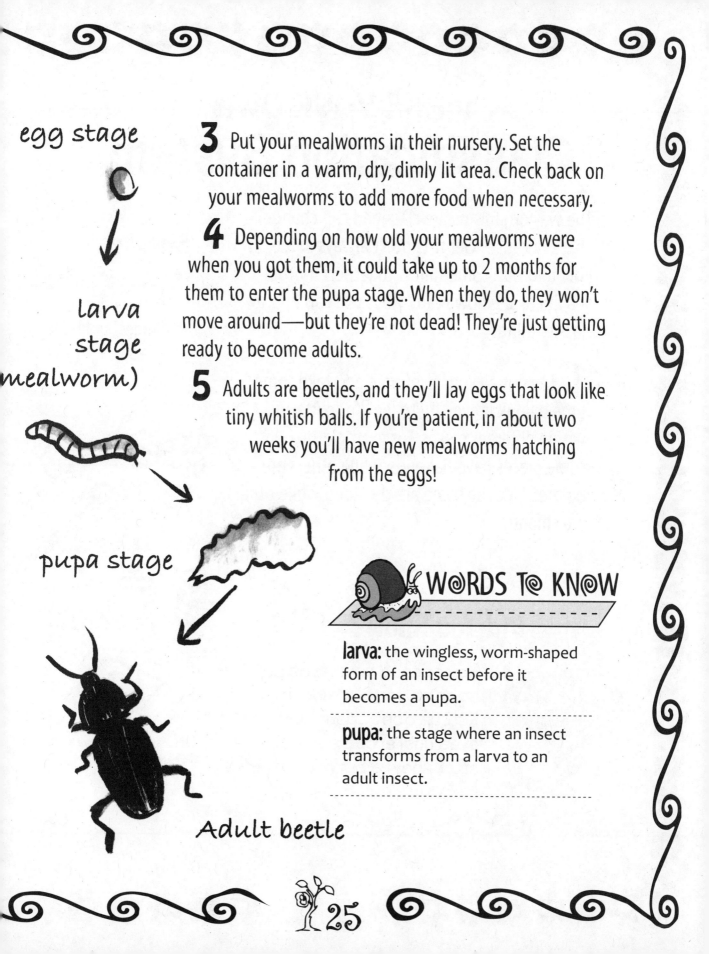

larva
stage
(mealworm)

pupa stage

Adult beetle

3 Put your mealworms in their nursery. Set the container in a warm, dry, dimly lit area. Check back on your mealworms to add more food when necessary.

4 Depending on how old your mealworms were when you got them, it could take up to 2 months for them to enter the pupa stage. When they do, they won't move around—but they're not dead! They're just getting ready to become adults.

5 Adults are beetles, and they'll lay eggs that look like tiny whitish balls. If you're patient, in about two weeks you'll have new mealworms hatching from the eggs!

WORDS TO KNOW

larva: the wingless, worm-shaped form of an insect before it becomes a pupa.

pupa: the stage where an insect transforms from a larva to an adult insect.

MAKE YOUR OWN
Classification System

The way organisms are classified can change. That's because scientists don't always agree on how to group some things together! Try this activity to see how many ways you can find to classify things.

Supplies

❁ assorted hardware such as screws, nails, hinges, and bolts

1 Lay out all your hardware and take some time to look it over. Try to look for patterns within different pieces. For example, do some pieces have flat ends, while others are pointed? Maybe some are threaded while others are smooth.

Did You Know?

You opened your eyes as soon as you were born. Kittens don't open their eyes until around a week after they're born.

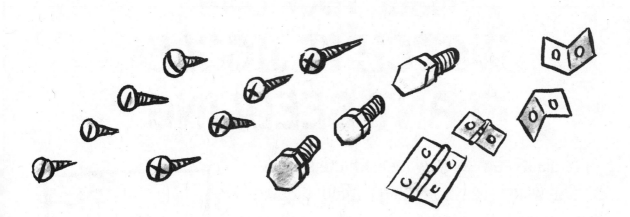

2 Once you've settled on some **similarities**, pile things together in groups based on your **observations**. Keep going until everything's sorted. Don't worry if some things don't seem to have anything in common with anything else—sometimes that happens with living organisms, too!

3 Afterwards, put everything back in a pile and see if you can come up with a completely different system. Maybe this time you can classify by size. Try asking a friend or someone in your family to classify the items into groups. See if their classification system is similar or totally different from yours.

WORDS TO KNOW

similarity: a way that two things are like each other.

observation: something you notice.

Activity

MAKE YOUR OWN
WATCH IT JIGGLE PLANT SEEDLING

Since plants start to grow beneath the soil, it's hard to watch seeds sprouting without digging them up. By using gelatin instead of soil you can actually see the plants begin to develop!

1 Mix the gelatin according to the package directions. You only need one packet, and you'll have some left over.

2 Pour the gelatin into the baby food jar. You don't need to fill it all the way—about an inch is fine. To feed your plant, add two drops of liquid house plant fertilizer.

Supplies

❀ plain gelatin
❀ very clean baby food jar
❀ liquid house plant fertilizer
❀ seeds—bean seeds grow quickly, but you can use any seed you have available

3 Let the gelatin cool and firm up. When it's ready, drop a seed or two on top of the gelatin.

4 Place the jar in a sunny place and check it every day to watch the plant grow. You can draw pictures every couple of days to record the progress.

Activity

MAKE YOUR OWN
YEAST EXPERIMENT

If you've ever made bread, you're familiar with yeast. These tiny tan balls with a strong smell look like just another nonliving thing such as flour or sugar. But yeast is actually part of the fungus family, like mushrooms. Using this experiment, you can feed the yeast and see how it gives off carbon dioxide gas.

1 Pour the water into the soda bottle. Add the sugar and put the top on the bottle. Shake the bottle until the sugar is dissolved. Add the package of yeast and shake some more.

2 Take off the top. Stretch the opening of the balloon over the end of the soda bottle. Wait about an hour. When you return, you'll find the balloon is inflated.

What's happening?

The balloon filled with a gas called carbon dioxide. The yeast is an organism that eats the sugar. It produces the gas as a result. Plain old flour can't do that!

Supplies

* 1 cup warm water
* empty, clean 2-liter soda bottle, with top
* 2 tablespoons sugar
* package of yeast
* balloon

29 *Activity*

MAKE YOUR OWN
POWER OF
SEEDS EXPERIMENT

It's amazing that something so small and delicate as a seed can survive to grow into a large plant. In this experiment, you'll see how strong seedlings really are. They have to be strong. Seeds need to push through the ground, and through or around anything that might be blocking their path!

Supplies
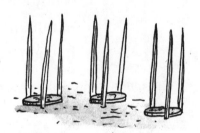

❁ small container
❁ soil
❁ bean seeds
❁ pennies
❁ toothpicks
❁ water

1 Fill the small container with soil. Make some small hollows in the surface, and drop a seed into each one. Cover the seeds with soil.

2 Place a penny on top of each seed's location. Carefully push three toothpicks around the outside of each penny. Don't push down on the coins. You're just making guides for each penny.

3 Place your container in a warm, sunny location. A windowsill is a good spot. Keep your seeds watered and warm.

4 When the seeds start to sprout, watch carefully. Do you think the pennies are too heavy for the little seedlings? You'll see the seedlings push the pennies upward along their toothpick guides as they grow.

Activity ❁ 30

HERE COMES BABY!

When the sun comes up in the morning, you get out of bed and go through your usual routine. You eat breakfast and brush your teeth. It's the start of a new day.

When a new organism is made, it's like the beginning of a new day. Babies in each classification group start their lives the same way as other babies in that group. It's like their morning routine. A baby robin starts its life the same way as a baby cardinal or rooster. It pecks its way out of its egg, kicks away the shell, and lifts its wobbly head up to find food.

But babies belonging to other groups may have very different beginnings. After all, you know that elephants don't lay eggs. Can you imagine the size THAT egg would be? And you weren't born in a pond, able to breathe under water. Here's how some different organisms each begin life.

HELLO, WORLD!

Before you were born, you grew in a safe place inside your mom's body. That's the same way kittens, zebras, goats, gorillas, cows, and just about all the other mammals grow, too.

Some mammals give birth to more than one baby at a time. Cats usually have a **litter** of around five kittens. Sometimes there are more, sometimes less. Mice have litters of five to ten babies.

WORDS TO KNOW

litter: a group of babies born at the same time.

gestation period: the length of time a mother carries a baby inside her.

marsupial: a mammal whose babies grow in a pouch on the mom after they are born.

echidna: a small, ant-eating monotreme.

The length of time a mammal carries her baby is called the **gestation period**. This is different from creature to creature. In humans, it's nine months. For killer whales, it's around a year and a half. And for mice it's only about 20 days!

WE ARE UNUSUAL... WE ARE MARSUPIAL (AND MONOTREME)

Not all baby mammals grow inside the mom's body, though. There are two kinds of mammals that do things a little differently.

Marsupials give birth after a much shorter gestation period than many other mammals. The baby isn't ready to live outside the mother yet. So after it's born, a marsupial makes its way to a special pouch on the mom. Kangaroos, koalas, opossums, and wombats are all marsupials.

Monotremes lay eggs. There aren't many kinds of mammals that are monotremes—just the platypus and two species of **echidna**. These are little animals that eat ants.

EGG-STREMELY DIFFERENT

Did You Know?

After the mother emperor penguin lays her egg, the father watches over it while the mother searches for food. The father holds the egg on top of his feet for four months. He never puts the egg down, not even to feed himself.

Eggs are pretty amazing. They're little mini-homes for developing animals. Eggs have everything a growing baby needs—protection, food, and room to grow.

Birds, reptiles, amphibians, and fish all begin life inside eggs. But all eggs aren't made the same. There are many differences.

BIRD EGGS

The first thing you notice about a bird's egg is that it has a hard outer shell. Just underneath that shell is a **membrane**. This layer protects the developing chick against harmful outside germs. Inside the membrane is the part you'd call the egg white. Its real name is **albumen**, and its main job is to protect the egg yolk.

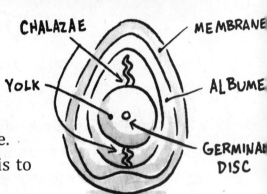

The yellow center of the egg is the yolk. The yolk is held in place by two squiggly string-type anchors called **chalazae** (sounds like "chuh-lazy"). In the very center of the yolk is a light dot. This is called the germinal disc. It's what starts developing into a chick. As the baby bird develops, it uses the yolk for food.

Birds have to **incubate** their eggs. They sit on the eggs to keep them warm. If the egg doesn't stay warm enough, the chick won't develop properly. After a few weeks of growing, the chick is ready to hatch. It starts squirming around and pecks at the inside of the shell, finally popping open a little hole. The baby bird keeps pecking and pushing until it breaks out of its shell. The feathers are damp at first, but they dry in a few hours.

Did You Know?

The ostrich lays the largest egg. It can weigh up to four pounds!

REPTILES

Reptiles are another class of animals in the phylum chordata. They breathe air and have backbones, like mammals and birds. But reptiles are covered with scales or plates and are cold-blooded. This means they can't make their own body heat so they can't move when it's cold. Crocodiles, snakes, and turtles are all reptiles.

 WORDS TO KNOW

membrane: the thin, flexible layer inside an egg shell.

albumen: the clear, slimy substance inside an egg around the yolk.

chalazae: the "anchors" that hold the yolk suspended in the egg, in the albumen.

incubate: to keep a developing egg warm.

REPTILE EGGS

Like bird eggs, reptile eggs have a membrane, white, yolk, and chalazae. They can be hard like birds' eggs, or tough and leathery. Some reptiles lay their eggs and leave them, while others guard their eggs. Crocodiles will help their young hatch, gently easing them out of their shells. All turtles, tortoises, and crocodiles lay eggs. So do many snakes and lizards, like iguanas and geckos.

But not all reptiles lay eggs. Some kinds of lizards, chameleons, and snakes give birth to live young. Inside the mom, they're attached to a yolk and surrounded by a clear membrane. When they're born, they have to break out of that membrane.

AMPHIBIAN EGGS

Amphibians lay their eggs outside of their body, and then they usually don't have anything else to do with them. The eggs are small, jelly-like masses with a tiny dark spot that is the developing baby. Amphibian eggs are laid in large numbers, all clumped together. Sometimes they look like a foamy blob. The babies inside develop into tadpoles. When they're ready, they squirm out into the water. The yolk that was left over is attached to their body, like a big belly. Tadpoles eat the yolk until it's gone.

MY MOM HAD 200 BABIES

Why do some animals, like frogs, mice, and insects, have so many babies at one time? It's because these organisms have a lot of **predators**. What would happen if a mouse only had one or two babies, and a hawk came along and gobbled them up? Very soon, there would be almost no mice left. Plants produce many seeds at once because some seeds get eaten. And some seeds might not land where they can grow.

In order to keep the species going, some plants and animals have to produce dozens—or even millions!—of offspring, spores, or seeds every year.

WORDS TO KNOW

predator: an animal who eats other animals or plants.

Did You Know?

Some sea stars can lose one of their arms, and that arm can grow into a whole new organism!

FISH EGGS

Fish eggs are soft and squishy and look like they have clear jelly inside. Various species of fish eggs develop differently. The most common is when the eggs grow and develop outside the mom's body, the way birds' eggs do. Also like birds, babies get their food from the yolk inside the egg. But unlike birds, who look like little adults, fish look like little tadpoles when they hatch. After a short time in this stage, they change and start looking like the adult fish of their species.

Another way fish can develop is when the eggs hatch and continue developing inside the mom's body. Again, they use the yolk for nutrition. When they're born, they're past the "tadpole" stage and are already like small versions of their species. Guppies and some shark species develop this way.

LIFE INSIDE A SEED

And what about plants? You know they grow from seeds. But just how does that work?

Inside the seed is a tiny plant, ready to grow. Like an egg, a seed has food stored inside and a hard, protective shell. But how does the seed know when to start growing? When it gets warmth and water!

First, the protective shell cracks open and roots start pushing downward. Then the stem of the plant begins uncurling upward, pushing through the soil. Once it has broken through the dirt, the plant stem begins growing larger. Soon it adds leaves.

WORDS TO KNOW

gravitropism: how a plant responds to the force of gravity. Roots grow downward and leaves grow upward. Gravity is the pull toward the center of the earth.

Plants know which direction is up and which is down. **Gravitropism** makes sure the plant has a good shot at living. Otherwise, many seeds would never find their way out of the ground!

SPORE OR SEED?

What's the difference between a spore and a seed? One big difference is that spores don't have a lot of food stored inside them, like a seed does. Seeds are also bigger than spores. You'd need a microscope to see some spores—they're that tiny!

HEY, YOU'RE A FUNGI!

Fungi might seem like they should be a part of the plant kingdom. But, fungi don't make their own food using sunlight. They're part of nature's cleanup crew. Fungi break down things like rotting logs or animal waste.

And fungi don't reproduce like green plants, either. Instead of seeds, fungi release spores. These spores are found on places like the underside of the mushroom cap. That's why the mushroom sticks up above the ground— to release the spores that make new mushrooms.

MAKE YOUR OWN
TOPSY-TURVY PLANT

When a plant first starts growing out from a seed, it always sends its roots down and its shoot up. You can see this at work with this experiment.

1 Fill the small cup with the potting soil. Plant the bean seed and cover with more soil. Keep moist and wait a few days until the bean seed has sprouted and formed a tiny seedling.

Supplies

❀ small cup
❀ potting soil
❀ bean seed
❀ 2 sponges
❀ water
❀ string

2 Soak the 2 sponges in water until they're completely wet. If they're dripping, wring them out a little bit.

3 Gently remove the bean seedling from the cup. Carefully shake off most of the soil from its roots.

4 Lay the roots of the seedling between the 2 sponges, so that they are sandwiched between them. Make sure the shoot of the plant is sticking out.

5 Then tie the sponges together firmly with the string.

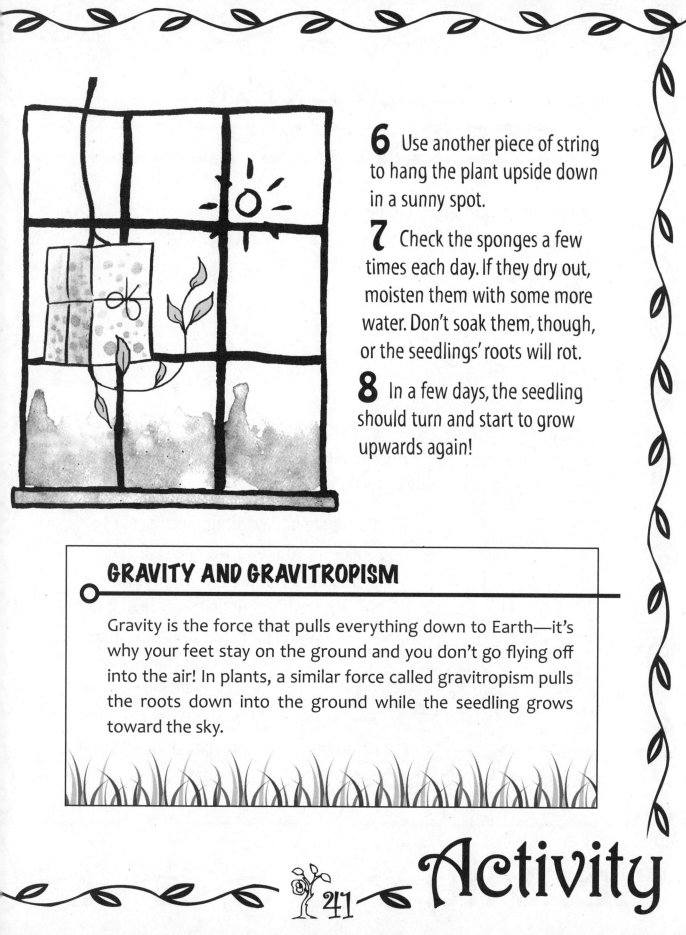

6 Use another piece of string to hang the plant upside down in a sunny spot.

7 Check the sponges a few times each day. If they dry out, moisten them with some more water. Don't soak them, though, or the seedlings' roots will rot.

8 In a few days, the seedling should turn and start to grow upwards again!

GRAVITY AND GRAVITROPISM

Gravity is the force that pulls everything down to Earth—it's why your feet stay on the ground and you don't go flying off into the air! In plants, a similar force called gravitropism pulls the roots down into the ground while the seedling grows toward the sky.

Activity

MAKE YOUR OWN
SEE-THROUGH EGG

Bird eggs are protected with a hard outer shell. In this project, you can see the inner membrane and even the yolk—without breaking the egg!

1 Place the egg in the bowl and cover it with vinegar. Let the egg sit in the vinegar for one to two days.

2 After a couple of days, drain the vinegar and check on your egg. The shell will have dissolved completely away, leaving you with a rubbery egg. Hold it up to the light. You should be able to see the yolk. The yolk is where the baby chicken grows if the egg isn't prepared for a person to eat.

Activity  42

MAKE YOUR OWN
SPORE PRINT

A mushroom cap has little gill-like dividers that hold the spores. In this project, you'll be able to make a cool picture with the spores! Look for a variety of mushrooms in the store—such as white button, shiitake, portabella, or oyster mushrooms. **NOTE: Only pick wild mushrooms with an adult who knows which ones are safe because some are quite poisonous. Always wash your hands very well after handling mushrooms.**

Supplies

❀ mushroom with a large cap (a wild mushroom in late summer or early fall gives the best print)
❀ scissors
❀ white paper
❀ glue stick
❀ large bowl
❀ hairspray (optional)

1 Gently remove the mushroom cap from the stem. If it doesn't pop right off, cut it with a pair of scissors.

2 Cover an area in the middle of your paper with the glue stick. It should be just larger than your mushroom cap. Lay the mushroom cap, gill side down, on top of the glued area.

3 Cover your mushroom cap with the bowl and leave it overnight.

4 Remove the bowl and mushroom. You'll find the spores have made a beautiful pattern on your paper. You can use the hairspray to coat the print, making it last longer.

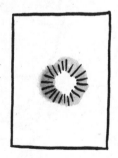

43 **Activity**

MAKE YOUR OWN
UNDERWATER VIEWER

A lot of life cycles happen under water, where you can't see them. With this underwater viewer you'll be able to get a peek at the action. Have an adult with you when you use this viewer near any body of water.

1 Use a can opener to remove both ends if you're using a metal can. If the edges are not smooth, cover them with duct tape. If you're using a milk carton, cut off both ends with the scissors. And if you're using a milk jug, cut off the neck and the bottom—you'll use the bottom as the viewer and look through the neck.

2 Wrap a sheet of plastic wrap over the bottom opening of your viewer. Stretch it tight enough so that it's smooth, but not so tight that it tears. Leave enough plastic wrap to go well up the sides of your viewer.

3 Using duct tape, tightly secure the plastic wrap to the sides of your viewer. Make sure you don't leave any open gaps, or water will seep through.

4 With an adult, go to the edge of a body of water. You can lie down alongside the water.

5 Put the plastic-wrapped end of the viewer into the water. Push it down far enough so that you can get a clear view of things, but not so far that water gushes over the top edge. Look into your viewer. Can you see fish? Tadpoles? Be patient. Sometimes if you stay very still, critters will come into view. Remember what you see. If you're not familiar with what you're seeing, ask an adult, or look it up when you get home.

Activity

GROW BABY, GROW!

Have you ever pulled on a favorite pair of jeans—only to find that your ankles are sticking out an inch below the hem? That's because you're in the growing stage of your life cycle.

After organisms come into the world, they start to change. Sometimes the changes are dramatic—like a caterpillar transforming into a moth. And sometimes the only change is in size.

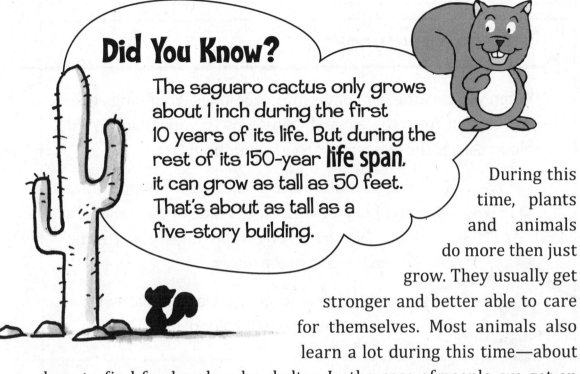

Did You Know?

The saguaro cactus only grows about 1 inch during the first 10 years of its life. But during the rest of its 150-year **life span**, it can grow as tall as 50 feet. That's about as tall as a five-story building.

During this time, plants and animals do more then just grow. They usually get stronger and better able to care for themselves. Most animals also learn a lot during this time—about how to find food and make shelter. In the case of people, we get an education—we learn to read and how to do lots of different things!

CHANGING BY LEAPS AND BOUNDS

Amphibians are masters of change. Not only do they change in appearance—they actually change from animals that breathe under water to animals that breathe on land.

W⊚RDS T⊚ KN⊚W

life span: the average expected length of time from birth to death for a species.

You've learned that frogs hatch out of their squishy eggs as tadpoles. For about a week they feed on the yolk that's on their bellies. Then they start swimming around, eating algae. They use gills to breathe underwater.

HOW DO GILLS WORK?

When you breathe, air comes into your lungs. Your lungs take the oxygen from the air and transfer it to your blood. Your blood carries the oxygen all around your body.

Fish and tadpoles have gills instead of lungs. Gills are feathery tissues on the sides of an animal's head. Gills have tiny veins that absorb the oxygen that's in the water.

Both lungs and gills get an animal what it needs—oxygen to its blood!

After about six weeks, tiny back legs sprout and the tadpole's body starts getting longer. Then tiny front legs pop out, elbow first. The tadpole's lungs are developing, too.

After about 3 months, the tadpole's tail starts shrinking. Now the tadpole looks like a really tiny frog. When it's ready, the young frog makes its way out of the water and starts living its life on land.

 WORDS TO KNOW

nymph: an insect that, when hatched, looks like a tiny version of an adult.

DOES THIS BUG YOU?

Most insects change a lot during the growing stage. They transform dramatically from the time they hatch—changing their size, shape, and color. These insects go through four growth steps.

But there are some insects that don't change much at all. They just get bigger. They shed their outer skin as they get too big for it. These kinds of insects only go through three growth steps.

3-Stage Growth Process

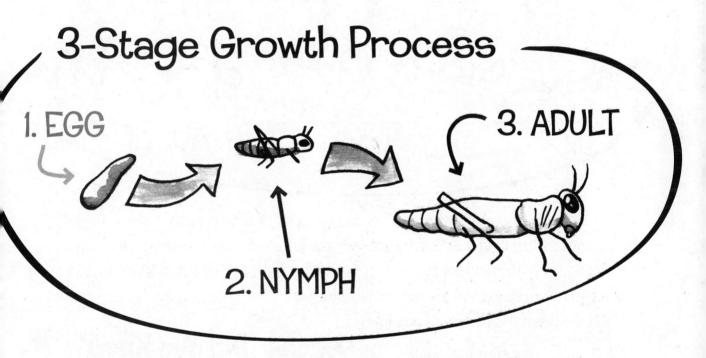

1. EGG

2. NYMPH

3. ADULT

When these insects emerge from their eggs, they look just like an adult—only much, much smaller. This is called the **nymph** stage. As these insects grow, they shed their skin whenever it gets too small, like a snake does. Crickets, grasshoppers, and praying mantes go through a nymph stage.

But what about the other insects that have a four-stage growth process? They emerge from their eggs as worms or caterpillars called larvae. These young insects have completely different body systems than the adults they will become. A larva eats a lot to get enough energy to make the transformation that's coming up.

4-Stage Growth Process

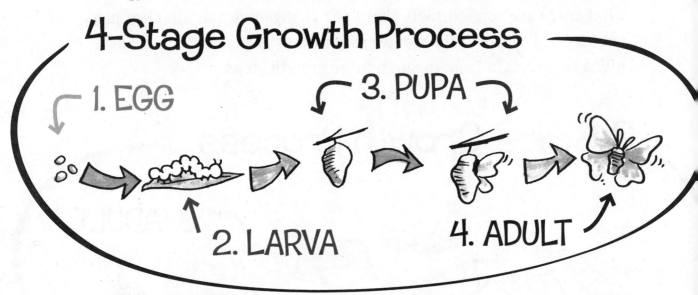

1. EGG

2. LARVA

3. PUPA

4. ADULT

Next is the pupa stage. This stage can be a very short time in an insect's life cycle, or it can last over a whole season. During the pupa stage, it's almost like the insect is in **hibernation**. Usually tucked inside a protective case, the insect finishes its transformation into an adult.

You're probably most familiar with a cocoon. This is the silk case that protects a moth pupa. A butterfly pupa is protected by a covering called a chrysalis.

Did You Know?

The pupa stage can last from a week to many months if the conditions in the environment are not just right. The insect waits to emerge.

YOU'RE CROWDING ME!

Every living thing is "programmed" to go through its life cycle in a certain way. But sometimes things in the **environment** affect those life cycles.

Bass are a kind of fish that live in lakes. If the lake doesn't have enough predators, the bass population can grow too large. If there are too many bass, there won't be enough food to feed them all. The bass will suffer from **stunted growth**.

Plants are the same way. If you keep a house plant in a pot too long, it gets "pot bound." This means its roots don't have room to spread out and grow. The plant ends up smaller than it should be. Sometimes trees in the forest can't grow very tall because they're too crowded or blocked from the sun by other trees.

WORDS TO KNOW

hibernation: a period of time when an animal is not active, eating, or moving around much.

environment: everything in nature, living and nonliving, including plants, animals, soil, rocks, and water.

stunted growth: when an organism doesn't grow as large as it should.

Did You Know?

The tallest tree in the world is the California redwood. It can grow up to 385 feet tall. That's taller than the Statue of Liberty!

HOW'S THE WEATHER?

Have you ever waited all winter to eat your first juicy handful of sweet, plump strawberries—only to find them all tiny and sour? That's because the weather conditions weren't right for the life cycle of the strawberry plants.

Some plants need a lot of spring rain to produce their fruits and vegetables. Others need hot summers. Some need cooler temperatures. A late frost can knock out many plants. It can stunt their growth, limit their food production, or even kill them.

Did You Know?

Monarch butterflies travel from North America to Mexico every year to wait out the cold winter. They fly up to 2,700 miles to get there!

52

Grow Baby, Grow!

When the weather turns cooler in the autumn, many animals change their behavior. They may start eating more, or eat fattier foods. That's because they know that food is going to be harder to find during the winter. They are stocking up.

Some animals eat as much as they can because they're going into hibernation for the winter. During hibernation they sleep a lot and don't move around much. They hardly eat anything—if at all.

For the black bear, the winter is also the time when they give birth. The babies spend their first months growing. They stay tucked in their warm den while snow swirls outside.

FUNGUS AMONG US

As they look for a place to grow, fungi spores drift around the environment—even inside a very clean home. What are they looking for? A surface that's damp and dark. Mold can feed off of food, but also things like wood, paper, and even inside old shoes! One spore will land, and then as it feeds, it branches out over the surface, kind of like frost crystals spreading.

MAKE YOUR OWN
STUFFED COCOON PIZZA

Supplies

✿ oven
✿ pizza dough
✿ fillings such as pepperoni, ham bits, pineapple, olives, peppers, mushrooms, hamburger
✿ cheese
✿ pizza sauce

Discovering what's inside a cocoon is exciting. Serve your family this cocoon pizza for a surprise dinner one night. You can tell them all about how a caterpillar transforms inside it.

1 Preheat the oven according to the directions for the pizza dough.

2 Pull off fist-sized chunks of pizza dough and roll them into flat ovals, however long you want your cocoons to be. You may want to have one cocoon per person. That way, you can fill each one according to everyone's taste. You can also fill each one differently and let everyone be surprised with what kind of "butterfly" comes out of their cocoon!

3 Pile the fillings and a little cheese and sauce on one half of each cocoon. Make sure you're not filling your cocoons too full—just put a layer about twice as deep as you'd find on top of a regular pizza. Leave about an inch of dough around the filling.

4 Fold over one side of the dough. Pinch it to the opposite side, sealing the edges well so nothing leaks. Try to keep the cocoon shape. Repeat with all of your cocoons.

5 Brush the tops with some more sauce and sprinkle with a little more cheese.

6 Bake the cocoons according to the pizza dough directions. You may have to bake it just a little longer, since your cocoons are thicker than a traditional pizza. Just have an adult check to see if they're done.

7 When they're ready, serve your cocoons to your family. They'll have fun finding out what's in each cocoon!

MAKE YOUR OWN
MOLD GROWTH EXPERIMENT

Have you ever picked up a piece of bread and found a fuzzy green or white spot on it? That's mold, which is a fungus. Try this experiment to see what conditions are best for mold to grow in. This way, you'll never be surprised by mold on your sandwich again! Have a parent help with this one. Some people are allergic to certain molds. Be sure to wash your hands when you're done.

Supplies
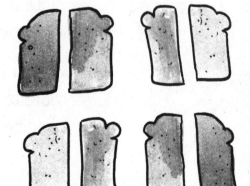

* four slices of bread
* plastic wrap
* paper bags
* water
* magnifying glass
* paper and pencil

1 Cut all the pieces of bread in half. For each test, you'll use two halves of bread.

2 For the first sample, wrap one bread half in plastic wrap, and leave the other out in the air. Put both of these samples on the kitchen counter.

3 For the second sample, put one bread half in a paper bag (or in the cupboard if you don't have a bag). Put the other half in direct sunlight, like on a windowsill.

4 For the third sample, spray one bread half lightly with water. You don't want it soaking wet, just a bit damp. Keep checking on it and spray it a little when it seems to dry out. Keep the other half dry, but in the same location (a different kitchen counter from the first sample is fine).

5 For the last sample, put one bread half in a warm, dark place. On top of the refrigerator in a paper bag will work well. Put the other half in a cold, dark place, such as inside the refrigerator in a paper bag.

6 Check on all your samples each day. Examine them carefully with a magnifying glass. Write down what you observe.

7 You'll find mold begins to grow on some of your samples:

SAMPLE ONE: does mold grow faster on the bread that's wrapped, or not wrapped?

SAMPLE TWO: does mold grow faster on the bread in the dark, or in the light?

SAMPLE THREE: does mold grow faster on the bread that is damp, or dry?

SAMPLE FOUR: does mold grow faster on the bread that is warm, or chilled?

Activity

MAKE YOUR OWN
IT'S CROWDED IN HERE! EXPERIMENT

Growing in crowded conditions affects both plants and animals. See for yourself with this simple experiment. You'll have to be patient! It can take a while to see the results, depending on the seeds you use.

1 Fill the pots with equal amounts of soil.

2 In the first pot, plant four seeds spaced well apart. Cover with a little soil, according to the directions on the seed packet.

3 In the second pot, sprinkle in a bunch of seeds. Depending on the size of the seed you're using, plant up to 20 or more. Cover with soil.

Supplies
❀ two small pots
❀ soil
❀ radish or other seeds
❀ water

pot with seeds with plenty of space

pot with crowded seeds

4 Water both pots and set them in a warm, sunny place. Care for each pot equally with water, making sure not to over water them or let them dry out.

What's happening?

Did the pots grow in the same way or did one grow better than the other? What are some differences between the plants in the two pots?

Keep it going:

If you have vegetable plants, you can keep this experiment going. Tend to them until they are ready to harvest. What do you find? How are the vegetables in the crowded pot different from the ones in the spaced pot? If you were to plant your own garden, which planting technique would you use? The crowed pot technique or the spaced one?

Activity

MAKE YOUR OWN
TREE MEASURING STICK

Want to find out how tall a tree is? Here's a way to do it—without getting out a ladder!

1 Measure your friend's height and write it down. Then, have your friend go stand next to the tree.

2 Stand far enough away from the tree so that you can see its top and bottom. Hold the stick out at arm's length and move it so the top of the stick is lined up with the top of your friend's head. Without moving the stick, use the pencil to make a mark on the stick where your friend's feet are.

THIS IS YOUR FIRST MARK, YOUR FRIEND'S HEIGHT.

Supplies

❀ measuring tape
❀ friend
❀ long stick such as a yardstick or broomstick
❀ pencil

Activity

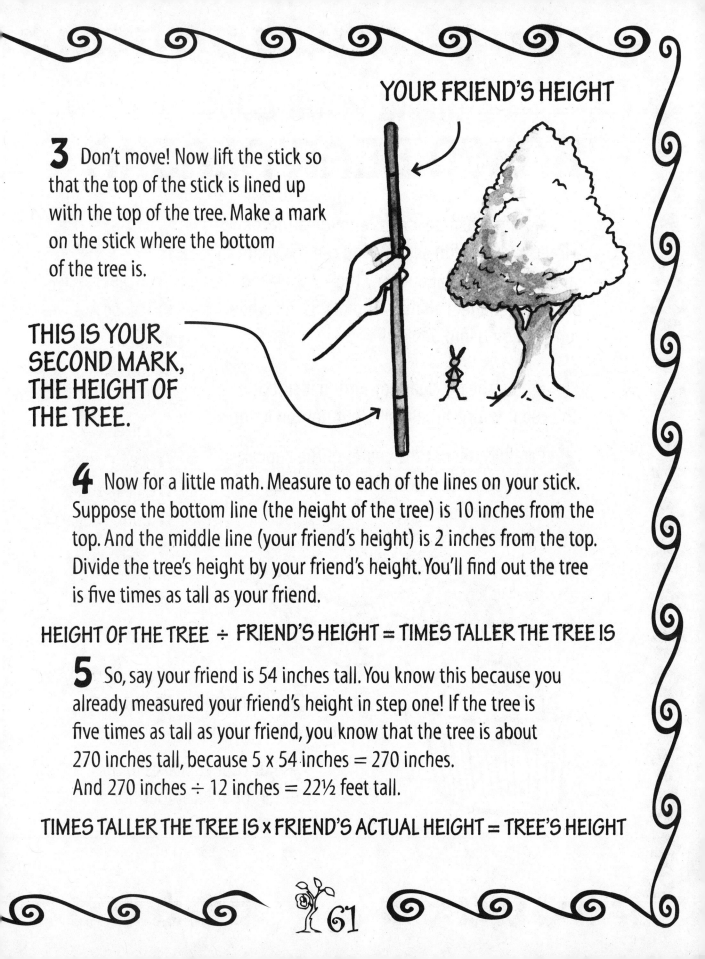

YOUR FRIEND'S HEIGHT

3 Don't move! Now lift the stick so that the top of the stick is lined up with the top of the tree. Make a mark on the stick where the bottom of the tree is.

THIS IS YOUR SECOND MARK, THE HEIGHT OF THE TREE.

4 Now for a little math. Measure to each of the lines on your stick. Suppose the bottom line (the height of the tree) is 10 inches from the top. And the middle line (your friend's height) is 2 inches from the top. Divide the tree's height by your friend's height. You'll find out the tree is five times as tall as your friend.

HEIGHT OF THE TREE ÷ FRIEND'S HEIGHT = TIMES TALLER THE TREE IS

5 So, say your friend is 54 inches tall. You know this because you already measured your friend's height in step one! If the tree is five times as tall as your friend, you know that the tree is about 270 inches tall, because 5 x 54 inches = 270 inches. And 270 inches ÷ 12 inches = 22½ feet tall.

TIMES TALLER THE TREE IS x FRIEND'S ACTUAL HEIGHT = TREE'S HEIGHT

MAKE YOUR OWN
BAKED BEAR ALASKA

It's amazing when bear cubs emerge after the winter. With this fun activity, you can tell your family and friends about how the seasons and the weather affect animals and plants. All while you're digging into dessert!

1 Soften the ice cream by letting it sit out on the counter for a little while (but not too long!).

2 Carefully dig out the center of the cupcakes using a spoon. Don't go all the way through to the bottom or sides.

Supplies
* ½ pint ice cream
* 4 cupcakes
* spoon
* freezer
* bowl
* mixer
* 4 egg whites
* ¼ cup sugar
* gummy bears
* oven

3 Fill the hollowed-out part with ice cream.

4 Put your cupcakes in the freezer for at least four hours.

5 Put the egg whites in a very clean bowl and whip them with a mixer until they're stiff. Continue to whip while adding the sugar. When they are fluffy, the egg white are ready.

6 Take the cupcakes out of the freezer, and set a couple of gummy bears on top of each one.

7 Spread the fluffy meringue over the cupcakes. Make sure to seal the entire top of the cupcake—you don't want any heat to reach the ice cream!

8 Set the cupcakes under a pre-heated broiler for three minutes, until the top is brown. Then dig in!

HIBERNATION

Certain animals deal with harsh winter conditions by hibernating. That's when they "sleep" for a long period of time. Their body temperature drops, their breathing slows down, and they don't eat or move much at all.

Activity

THE CYCLE CONTINUES

I magine someone baked you a batch of your favorite cookies. After gobbling them up, what if you found out that there could never be any more cookies? That wouldn't be good at all, would it?

That's why living things have a job to do once they're fully grown. They have to make sure life continues. The mushrooms in the forest, the snakes in the desert, the sea anemones in the ocean—they all have ways to create new life.

64

Adult organisms produce the seeds, spores, and eggs that create new life. But the ways that adults send these little packages of life out into the world are often very different from each other.

WORDS TO KNOW

disperse: to scatter something over a wide area.

BLOWING IN THE WIND

It's fun to blow on dandelions and watch the white fluff scatter everywhere, isn't it? Look closely and you'll see a little seed hanging from each white "parachute." By blowing these seeds around, you're helping to create new plants. When kids aren't around to blow on the seeds, the wind **disperses** them.

You also might have played with the little seed packages that maple trees drop. These packages use wings to disperse seeds! They are those little "helicopters" you can toss in the air to watch spiral down to the ground.

Did You Know?

The largest seed in the world is from the coco de mer palm tree. It's about 3 feet wide! This tree grows on the Seychelle Islands in the Indian Ocean.

After a walk through the forest you might find sticky burrs clinging to your socks. That's another way plants spread their seeds. Inside those prickly outer shells are the seeds to a plant.

Did You Know?

The average life span of a cat is 15 years. But a cat named Creme Puff in Texas lived to be 38! She holds the record for the oldest cat.

Other plants might depend on an animal to eat their seeds! If an animal eats berries from a bush it also eats the seeds in the berries. Those seeds come out in the animal's waste. The seeds might start a new plant right there.

Some plants, such as strawberry plants, send out runners to create new life. These are long, thin shoots sent out from the main plant. When the shoot touches the ground it starts a new little plant just like the adult. Sometimes one runner makes many plants.

CIRCLE OF LIFE

Everything in nature is a cycle. When something dies, the remains are often used to help other organisms live. **Scavenger organisms** are nature's clean-up crew. They usually don't cause the death of another animal or plant, but they do consume it once it has died.

Perhaps you've seen really large birds on the side of the road after an animal has been killed by a car. They could be turkey vultures that come to "clean up." Or you may have seen a line of ants parading back and forth to a dead grasshopper. They're using it for food.

WORDS TO KNOW

scavenger organism: an animal, bird, or other organism that eats dead animals or rotting food.

compost bin: a container where dead organisms break down.

microorganisms: living things so small you need a microscope to see them.

Fungi do the same thing. Mushrooms form on rotting logs or animal waste, cleaning it up. Nothing goes to waste in nature.

You may know what a **compost bin** is. You may even have one in your backyard. You put kitchen waste like fruit and vegetable scraps or coffee grounds into the compost bin. Then worms, beetles, and **microorganisms** begin the process of breaking that material down. In the end, you have soil material that you can spread on your garden to help it grow. The life cycle begins all over again.

Did You Know?

Dung beetles feed on animal waste. They gather it up into a ball and roll it away to eat later.

FINAL ACT

Once a living thing has completed its entire life cycle, it dies. Creatures like parrots and tortoises take a very, very long time to live out their lives. Some types of parrots can live over 100 years. Some tortoises live 150 years—or more!

But other creatures have very short life spans. The mayfly is an insect that lives in the water. It can live as briefly as 30 minutes!

But living things aren't guaranteed to fully live out their life span. Animals that are delicious to other animals—like mice—don't always reach old age. A lot depends on how healthy an organism is. A lot depends on the conditions of its environment. A little bit of luck helps too.

Here are some average life spans:

ELEPHANT	CATFISH	EAGLE	CHIMPANZEE
70 years	60 years	55 years	40 years

COBRA	WOLF	GREEN FROG	RABBIT
28 years	18 years	10 years	9 years

FOREVER IS A LONG TIME

No living thing lasts forever. But scientists have discovered that some organisms have the special ability to almost succeed in living forever.

Hydra are tiny animals less than a quarter of an inch long that live in fresh water. They have a very simple body. A hydra looks kind of like a very skinny sea star with a tiny trunk. Scientists believe hydra do not age at all. So it's possible a hydra could keep living forever.

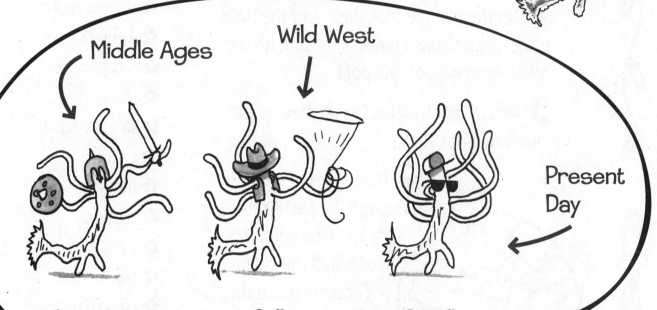

Middle Ages

Wild West

Present Day

The History of "Joe-Hydra"

There is also a type of tiny jellyfish that can possibly live forever. This animal can go back and forth between two life stages. If one of these jellyfishes doesn't get eaten or die for some other reason, it could keep it going back and forth and never die.

MAKE YOUR OWN
HANGING JELLYFISH

Here's a jellyfish that will "live" as long as you keep it hanging around! **Have an adult help you with boiling the flour and water.**

1 In a pot, mix together the flour and water. Bring the mixture to a boil on the stove, stirring well.

2 Let the mixture cool, then pour the flour paste into a shallow bowl. Make sure it's cool, or else your balloon will pop!

3 Inflate your balloon. Cut the newspaper into long strips.

4 Drag strips of paper through the paste and drape them smoothly over half the balloon. Continue doing this until the entire half of the balloon is covered. Don't lay your strips on too thick— two layers is plenty.

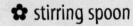

Supplies
❀ pot
❀ stirring spoon
❀ 1 cup flour
❀ 5 cups water
❀ stove
❀ shallow bowl
❀ balloon
❀ newspaper
❀ scissors
❀ paint
❀ paint brush
❀ crepe paper
❀ tape or glue
❀ string
❀ large needle

5 Let the balloon dry for several hours at least. It might need to dry overnight or even for a couple of days.

6 When the paper on the balloon is completely dry, pop the balloon. Pull the balloon away from the paper cap. This is your jellyfish. Paint your jellyfish whatever color you want, inside and out, and let it dry.

7 Cut very long strips of crepe paper. The strips should all be the same length. Tape or glue them around the inside of the jellyfish so they hang down like long tentacles.

8 Thread a long piece of string onto the needle and knot the end. From the inside of the jellyfish, poke the needle through the top of the jellyfish and bring the string all the way through. You can use this string to hang your jellyfish anywhere you like!

Did You Know?

You can make your jellyfish's tentacles as long as you want. The world's longest jellyfish has tentacles that are half the length of a football field!

Activity

MAKE YOUR OWN
LIFE IN A ROTTING LOG

When you're walking in the forest and see a rotting log, you're looking at the end of a tree's life cycle. That log is now helping other organisms live. If you look closer, you might see fungus and insects living on the log. You can recreate this little city of life, but be sure you have your parents' permission to do this project.

Supplies

✿ small log about 3 feet long and 6 inches thick
✿ water
✿ basin or bathtub
✿ blender
✿ 1 cup plain yogurt
✿ patch of moss about 4 inches long and wide

1 Soak your log in warm water for a day. Make sure it's fairly damp.

2 In an old blender, combine the yogurt with the moss. You want to make it pasty.

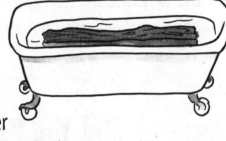

3 Set your log outside in a warm, shady area. Try to find a place that has a lot of other plants around it. Smear the green paste all over the log.

4 After a couple of days, moss should start to grow on your log. Fungus will begin to grow, and insects like ants will move in. You may find worms burrowing through the log as it rots. Keep checking on your log over time, and you'll find it is completely consumed.

Activity

72

MAKE YOUR OWN
SEED PARACHUTE

One way plants spread their seeds is by the wind. In this project, you can see for yourself how well this works.

1 Cut a square out of the tissue paper, about 6 inches on each side.

2 Put a piece of tape over each corner, then poke a hole through the tape with the needle. The tape will keep the corners from tearing.

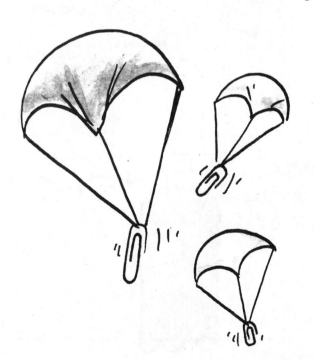

3 Tie a piece of string to each corner of the tissue paper.

4 Gather the ends of the string together and tie them to at least one paper clip.

5 Find a place with a good breeze, or turn on a fan inside. Release your parachute and see how far your "seed" travels.

Activity

MAKE YOUR OWN
MINI COMPOST BIN

Composting helps cut down on the amount of waste that ends up dumped in landfills. It also is good for the environment where you spread it—it helps keep nutrients in the ground and fertilizes plants.

Supplies
❀ 2-liter bottle
❀ black spray paint
❀ scissors
❀ nail
❀ shredded newspaper or dry leaves
❀ coffee grounds, egg shells, or chopped vegetable scraps
❀ water
❀ duct tape

1 Remove the label from the bottle and rinse it out well. Put the cap on tightly.

2 Cover the outside of the bottle with black paint and let it dry completely.

FSSSSS

3 Cut a door in the side of the bottle, about 5 inches tall by 3 inches wide. Leave one long side attached to the bottle so it can swing open and shut.

4 Have an adult use a nail to poke holes all around the bottle. The holes should cover the bottle.

5 Open the door and add about 3 inches of shredded paper or crunched-up dried leaves. On top of that, lay your food scraps. Wet everything down until it's damp, but not soaking wet. Close the door and seal it with duct tape.

6 Set your bin in a sunny place. Check it every day to make sure it's not too wet or too dry. If it's too wet, take the cap off to let it air out a little.

7 Once a day, roll the bottle back and forth a couple of times to mix everything and add air. In about a month, you'll have compost to use for your garden or potted plants!

Activity

THREATS TO LIFE CYCLES

You're in your backyard, playing with your friend, and you get hungry. You know where to go. Just walk into your house and head to the kitchen. You might grab an apple from a bowl on the table, or maybe make yourself a sandwich.

When it rains, you're safe and dry inside your house, too. Your home is like your habitat, the place where you find food and shelter. Each living thing has its own ideal habitat, too. Palm trees grow well in warm places. Polar bears are perfectly made for freezing Arctic weather. And sharks thrive in the ocean. In a perfect world, all living things would live in their habitats without any trouble. But in real life, things happen.

It can get too hot or too dry for plants to grow. Or habitats can be destroyed. If trees get cut down, birds can't build nests there to lay their eggs.

THE FORECAST IS...

What kind of weather is perfect for you? Hot and sunny? Cold and snowy? Every living thing has "perfect" weather conditions to live in. But the weather is something no one can control.

Sometimes places have a **drought**. This is when it doesn't rain enough. Then plants and animals struggle to find the water they need to survive.

Plants can survive a drought by going **dormant**. This is kind of like going to sleep. They may turn yellow and look dead, but they're really just saving the water they have. A plant won't grow at all during this time. It's like the plant is just waiting patiently for the rain to come again.

During a drought, animals have to move around to find water as best they can. You can help by setting out birdbaths to help your feathered friends through a tough time. Make sure the water is no more than 3 inches deep.

WORDS TO KNOW

drought: a long period of time when it doesn't rain as much as usual.

dormant: a time when plants stop growing.

Did You Know?

In Africa and South America, a freshwater fish called a lungfish can survive the dry season. It burrows into mud and "sleeps" until the water comes again!

HEY! THAT WAS MY HOUSE!

Imagine coming home from school to find your house gone. Instead, a bunch of cows are now living in a field where your living room used to be. You'd be pretty shocked and upset!

Did You Know?

Some animals, like the Arctic fox, change the color of their coat to blend in with their surroundings. The Arctic fox has a white coat in the winter and a brown coat in the summer.

As the human population grows, we often take over land. Many animals and plants live on that land. When they lose their homes, it disrupts their life cycles. They no longer have a place to grow, find food, and have babies.

Animals are perfectly suited to their habitat. This is where they can find the food and the shelter they need. Sometimes an animal's body color matches its surroundings. When its habitat is destroyed, the animal stands out more. This makes it easier for predators to see—and catch—them.

protected habitat: an area that is kept the way it is to protect the plants and animals that live there.

endangered: a plant or animal with a very low population.

There are some places where the government steps in and says, "Nope. You can't destroy this area." This is called a **protected habitat**. It is usually protected because the plants or animals that live there are **endangered**. That means they have such a low population that destroying their home would put them at risk.

CLEAN UP NATURE'S ROOM

Sometimes life cycles are interrupted by a big old mess. Garbage that's dumped can kill plants. Animals that depend on those plants for food may struggle to survive. Or the garbage itself can hurt the animals. The plastic rings from a six-pack of soda can get caught around the necks of birds and other animals, choking them.

The chemicals humans use can have an effect on life cycles, too. **Pollutants** from factories and vehicles gather in the air above the earth. When it rains, those pollutants come raining down, too. This is called **acid rain**. Acid rain damages plants and pollutes the water.

DDT

After World War II, a chemical **pesticide** called DDT (short for a really long chemical name!) was used to kill insects in the fields of farms. After a while, though, people figured out that the chemical was also getting into the soil and water.

The fish that absorbed DDT were eaten by birds like the bald eagle, brown pelican, and peregrine falcon. When those birds laid their eggs, the chemical made their egg shells too thin to protect the chicks—and they died.

Scientists think that DDT caused the number of bald eagles to decline so much that they became endangered. Once DDT was made illegal, the bald eagle's numbers increased again. They have been removed from the endangered list.

In 2010, an oil well on the floor of the Gulf of Mexico near Louisiana ruptured. It released hundreds of thousands of gallons of oil into the water. The oil affected all marine life. Oil is very tough on plants and animals because it's so difficult to clean off.

WORDS TO KNOW

pollutants: waste material that damages the environment.

acid rain: rain polluted with acid that harms the environment.

pesticide: a chemical used to kill pests, such as insects.

WHERE'S MY BED?

Oysters live on sturdy reefs called oyster beds. These beds are made from oyster shells. But when too many oysters are fished, there aren't enough shells to maintain the beds.

This means that when baby oysters are born, they have nothing to cling to. So they drift away or get eaten by predators. Fortunately, people are starting to restore the oyster beds for future generations.

Eek! Don't let go!

MAKE YOUR OWN
HABITAT SURVIVAL CHALLENGE

Supplies

* candy-coated chocolate pieces from one large bag or two 14-ounce bags
* 6 plastic baggies
* 6 pieces of colored construction paper, 1 each in red, yellow, green, orange, brown, and white
* 1-3 friends or family members
* timer or stopwatch
* paper and pencil

Find out how habitat destruction can put some animals at risk. If animals don't blend in with their surroundings, it's easy for them to get gobbled up by predators—just like the helpless candy in this experiment!

1 Divide your candy into the smaller baggies. You need to put 10 of each of the following colors in each bag: red, yellow, green, orange, and brown. You'll end up with 50 pieces in each baggie.

Activity

2 Lay one of the pieces of construction paper down on the table. It doesn't matter which color you start with. Ask your volunteers to sit at the table.

3 Explain what your volunteers need to do. Using only two fingers of one hand, they need to pick up and eat all the candies they can until you say, "Stop." Their other hand must stay behind their back the whole time.

4 When everyone is ready, pour the candies from one of the baggies onto the paper. Tell your volunteers to begin, and start your timer. After 8 seconds, say, "Stop."

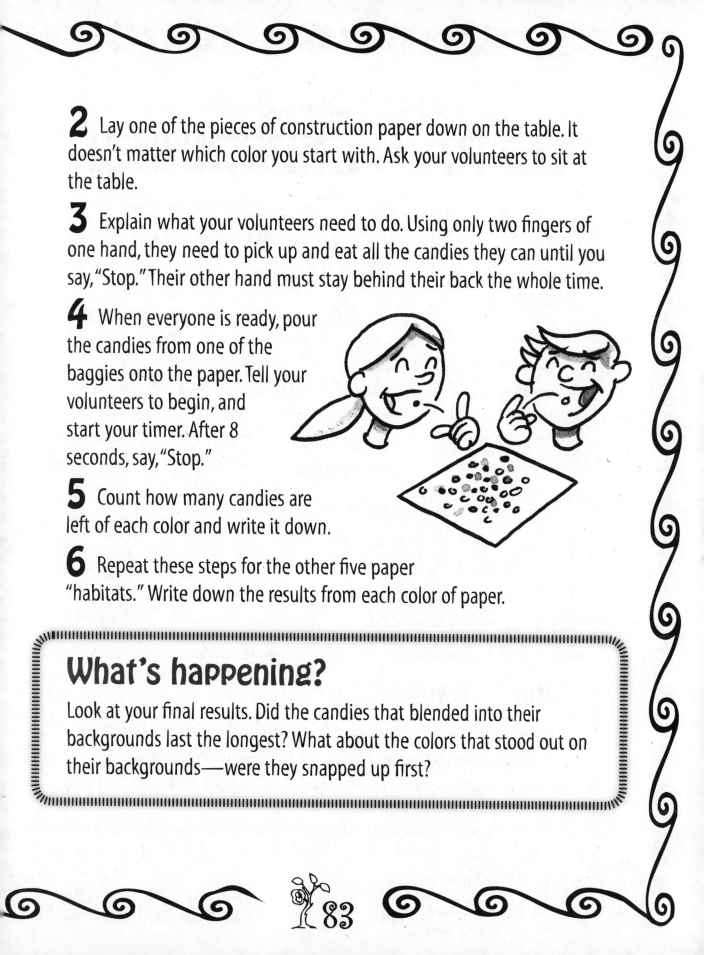

5 Count how many candies are left of each color and write it down.

6 Repeat these steps for the other five paper "habitats." Write down the results from each color of paper.

What's happening?

Look at your final results. Did the candies that blended into their backgrounds last the longest? What about the colors that stood out on their backgrounds—were they snapped up first?

MAKE YOUR OWN
ACID RAIN EXPERIMENT

Find out how "acid rain" affects plants. Distilled water has no acid in it, while vinegar is high in acid.

Supplies

❀ two identical small, potted plants

❀ marker

❀ distilled water

❀ 1 cup vinegar in a small bottle or old, rinsed milk jug

1 With the marker, label one pot "A" and one pot "B."

2 Add one cup of water to the vinegar so it's not quite as strong as plain vinegar.

3 Water plant A with distilled water, and plant B with the vinegar/water mix. The vinegar/water mix is your acid rain. Keep both plants in the same location. Do this for at least three days.

What's happening?

After about three days, can you see a difference? Plant A should be doing just fine, while plant B may be doing poorly. You can revive plant B by watering it with distilled water instead of the vinegar mix.

Activity 84

MAKE YOUR OWN
OIL SPILL EXPERIMENT

The 2010 oil spill in the Gulf of Mexico was the worst environmental disaster in America's history. Find out how tough it can be to clean up oil with this experiment.

1 Fill the bowl or pan halfway with water.

2 Pour the oil into the water. Stir with the spoon to create "waves." You can see how the oil doesn't mix with the water. This is just like a real oil spill.

3 Try to clean up the oil using a paper towel. Then, try circling the oil with yarn and dragging the oil off the water. Next, try the sponge. Finally, try using the detergent.

Supplies

* very large bowl or baking pan
* water
* ¼ cup cooking oil
* spoon
* paper towel
* yarn or string
* sponge
* dish detergent

What's happening?

Does any method work? It's easy to see the problems that clean-up crews face when trying to fix a real oil spill.

Activity

85

acid rain: rain polluted with acid that harms the environment.

albumen: the clear, slimy substance inside an egg around the yolk.

algae: a plant-like organism that turns light into energy but does not have leaves or roots.

antennae: a pair of organs on an insect's head that help it sense, or "feel," its surroundings.

aquatic: living or growing in water.

bacteria: tiny organisms found in animals, plants, soil, and water.

cells: the small units of a living thing.

chalazae: the "anchors" that hold the yolk suspended in the egg, in the albumen.

classify: to put things in groups based on what they have in common.

compost bin: a container where dead organisms break down.

disperse: to scatter something over a wide area.

dormant: a time when plants stop growing.

drought: a long period of time when it doesn't rain as much as usual.

echidna: a small ant-eating monotreme.

emu: a large bird with strong, fast legs that can't fly.

endangered: a plant or animal with a very low population.

environment: everything in nature, living and nonliving, including plants, animals, soil, rocks, and water.

forage: to search for food.

fungi: the plural of fungus.

GLOSSARY

gestation period: the length of time a mother carries a baby inside her.

gills: filter-like structures that let an organism get oxygen out of the water to breathe.

gravitropism: how a plant responds to the force of gravity. Roots grow downward and leaves grow upward. Gravity is the pull toward the center of the earth.

habitat: the natural area where a plant or an animal lives.

hibernation: a period of time when an animal is not active, eating, or moving around much.

incubate: to keep a developing egg warm.

larva: the wingless, worm-shaped form of an insect before it becomes a pupa.

life cycle: the full life of a living thing, from birth to death.

life span: the average expected length of time from birth to death for a species.

litter: a group of babies born at the same time.

marsupial: a mammal whose babies grow in a pouch on the mom after they are born.

membrane: the thin, flexible layer inside an egg shell.

metamorphosis: the process some animals go through in their life cycle. They change size, shape, and color.

microorganisms: living things so small you need a microscope to see them.

monotreme: a mammal that lays eggs.

nymph: an insect that, when hatched, looks like a tiny version of an adult.

observation: something you notice.

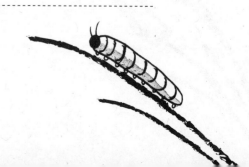

GLOSSARY

organism: a living thing, such as a plant or animal.

pesticide: a chemical used to kill pests, such as insects.

photosynthesis: how plants turn sunlight and water into food to grow.

phylum chordata: a large group in the animal kingdom. It includes mammals, birds, fish, reptiles, and amphibians. These animals all have spinal cords.

pollutants: waste material that damages the environment.

predator: an animal who eats other animals or plants.

protected habitat: an area that is kept the way it is to protect the plants and animals that live there.

pupa: the stage where an insect transforms from a larva to an adult insect.

scavenger organism: an animal, bird, or other organism that eats dead animals or rotting food.

similarity: a way that two things are like each other.

species: a group of plants or animals that are related and look the same.

stage: a single step in a process.

stunted growth: when an organism doesn't grow as large as it should.

RESOURCES

BOOKS

Aloian, Molly and Bobbie Kalman. *Life Cycle of a Flower.*
Crabtree Publishing Company (2004).

Fowler, Allan. *From Seed to Plant.* Children's Press (2001)

Hall, Margaret. *Hibernation.* Capstone Press (2008).

Kalman, Bobbie. *Animal Life Cycles.*
Crabtree Publishing Company (2009).

Kalman, Bobbie and Kathryn Smithyman. *The Life Cycle of a Frog.*
Crabtree Publishing Company (2006).

Thornhill, Jan. *I Found a Dead Bird: Kids' Guide to the Cycle of Life and Death.* Maple Tree Press (2006).

WEB SITES

National Geographic Kids: *http://www.kids.nationalgeographic.com*

The Children's Butterfly Site: *http://www.kidsbutterfly.org/life-cycle*

The Great Plant Escape: *http://urbanext.illinois.edu/gpe*

Web of Life at Kid's Planet: *http://www.kidsplanet.org/wol/index.html*

INDEX

INDEX

INDEX